delightfully
DURANGO

LOCAL CHEFS
SHARE GREAT RECIPES

PHOTOGRAPHY BY
McCarson L. Jones

Compiled by

DurangoMenu.com
Serving up *EVERY* menu in town.

Copyright © 2011 Durango Herald Small Press

ISBN 978-1-887805-34-6
Library of Congress Control Number: 2011929551

Photography: McCarson L. Jones
Design and Layout: Lisa Snider Atchison
Printing: CPC Solutions

www.thedurangoheraldsmallpress.com

A portion of the proceeds from the sale of this book goes to
THE WOMEN'S RESOURCE CENTER
in Durango, Colorado

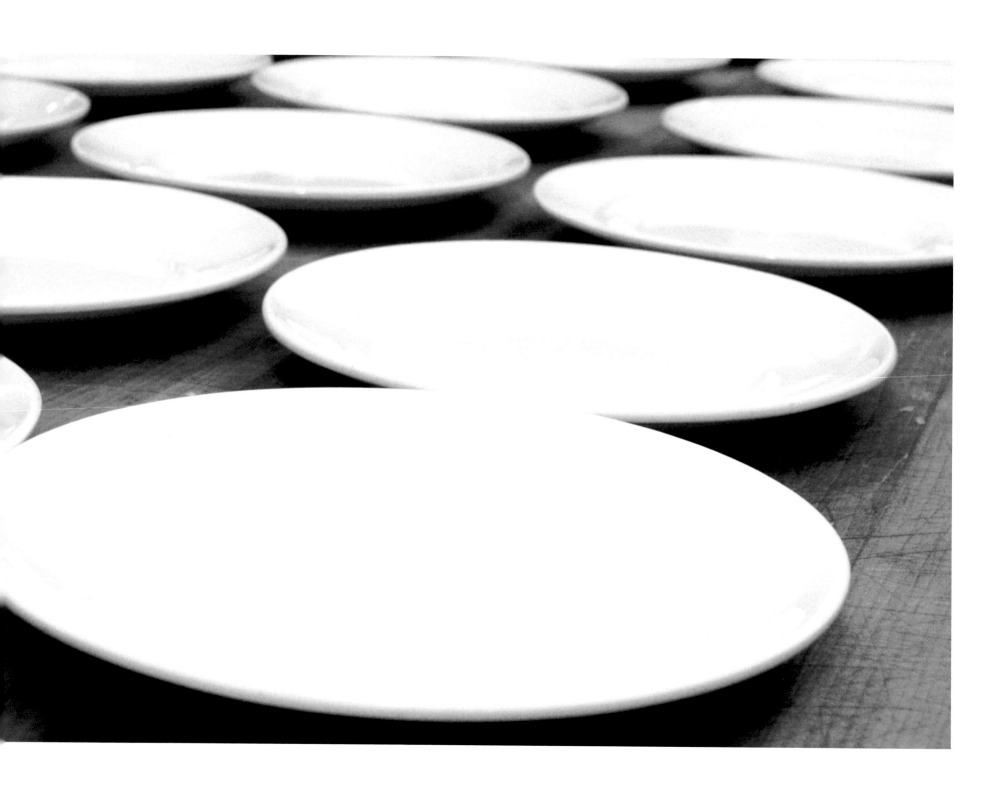

TABLE OF CONTENTS

ENTREES 41

DESSERTS 91

INDEX 101

PREFACE

The kernel of this book originated one evening over Mai Tais and Hand Grenades. The staff of Durango Menu talked of food and experiences of the palette. Durango is the kind of place, where the lovers of fine table fare can comfortably relive their youth by enjoying cultural dishes or break out into gustatory genres never before tasted.

Durango, Colorado, is rather like a port. It attracts a broad spectrum of the culinary world: entrepreneurs, laborers of flavor and grand chefs educated by elder cooks. It is an oasis of cuisine. Further, this is not a cookbook. It is a glimpse into cooking perfection.

As the night continued around the table, the Durango Menu team shared moments of dining and created a storybook image of their favorite dishes. They questioned the genesis of these meals, and how they evolved.

Recipes are coveted by their owners. Often times, they remain secret. Late nights hovering over a stove, and realizations found, are not easy shared. As the conversation continued into the weeks following, clandestine meetings were had with the purveyors of Durango's finest food. In short, you don't exist in this town unless you are that good. And the ones that are that good, and flourish here, will only release their ways if the listener is justified in asking for them.

This is a book of food – selection, preparation and plating – so that the one before the dish, with fork and knife in hand, can revel in its delight. The aromas waft and tell the taster there will be no experience better than this, at least for that night.

And with that, I am pleased to bring you *Delightfully Durango*. Many of these dishes I have savored. But even though I have been here for well over a decade, there are still ones within these pages that I haven't tried – that I am afraid to try, because I am not yet willing, to bring that experience I had at the chef's hand to my own kitchen. But I will. And I invite you to delve into this world of Durango Cuisine with me. If you have read this far, perhaps you are willing to go a bit further. This book is intended to bring the moments of Durango back home with you. Let it steep for a while and bring it out, when you need a taste of Durango. A taste of the world, from the Far East, the agaves of the South, Northeast to capes and beyond to Europe. And finally, southern blends of slowly smoked brisket.

These pages contain the collection of artisans' blood and sweat in the craft of food: Durango's finest revealed. That one evening, where it all started has become this. Not only so that you may read and learn from it, but also so that their own experiences can be noted and remembered. The sensation of good food leaves an impact that reaches beyond the moment. That evening of sitting over plates and drink, laughter, and anticipation created this publication. Some things are just too good to keep to yourself. There are some beauties too perfect to remain hidden.

– **Steve Linn**,
Manager of Sales & Operations of
DurangoMenu.com and Buzztown.com.

ESSENTIAL KITCHEN TOOLS & GADGETS

Durango Coffee Company

Of course the most essential ingredient in any kitchen is the cook. However, almost every cook will say that there are key kitchen tools that help make cooking more enjoyable and are essential for every kitchen. While there are literally thousands of kitchen gadgets available to help cooks make a great dinner, here we outline just a few of the essential gadgets that every cook will appreciate.

CHEF'S KNIFE

The most essential gadget or kitchen tool is the chef's knife. In this tool as in most tools, quality always pays off. So be certain to invest in a good knife. I really can't stress this enough. If you buy one of those cheap knife three-packs, your knives will be dull in a few months. So you'll go back and buy another cheap knife somewhere else, and the cycle will continue endlessly. Buying a large amount of cheap stuff will always cost more in the end than simply investing in something truly worthwhile to begin with. I swear by high quality Wusthof chef's knives. Other quality brands include Henckels or Global. The point is to buy something that will stay sharp, can be re-sharpened repeatedly, is comfortable in your hand and will last. A good chef's knife will truly be the investment of a lifetime and the most useful tool in your entire kitchen.

CUTTING BOARD

As the chef's knife is the most useful gadget in the kitchen it makes sense that a cutting board is the next most useful kitchen gadget, since it is very difficult to cut things without one. Invest in a nice cutting board and you can not only use it for its intended purpose, you can also use it as a nice serving piece at parties, at the dinner table or when you're serving an indoor picnic of cheese and fruit to your sweetheart. There are many different types and sizes of cutting boards, but I especially like the Epicurean brand. They are made of a unique wood composite, are very durable and elegant, and dishwasher safe, which is helpful in maintaining sanitary conditions.

MEASURING CUPS & SPOONS

This is really a no-brainer, but there are a few ways you can go wrong here. First, avoid cheap, plastic measuring spoons. In measuring very small amounts, it's easy to ruin a recipe by putting too much or too little into your batch of cookies. Get sturdy, well-made measuring spoons – they're always accurate and they'll last forever. When it comes to measuring cups, the same dictum applies. However, I recommend two sets of measuring cups, one for liquid and another for dry or solid measures. I like the great stainless steel dry measuring cups from RSVP and for liquids the four-cup angled measuring cup from OXO is pure genius.

TONGS

These are an extension of a cook's hands in the kitchen. I cannot overemphasize the extreme and varied usefulness of a pair of tongs. Once you own a good pair – preferably with silicone ends and a lock that allows them to stay shut when not in use – you'll wonder how you ever got by without them. Use them for turning a piece of meat in the pan, pulling a hot baking sheet towards you if it's gone too far back in the oven, serving and plating food...you get it. The possibilities are endless.

SPATULA

There are all manner of differently shaped spatulas available for your various culinary needs: omelet spatulas, fish spatulas, cookie spatulas, kitchen spatulas. But you really need to start with just one, and make it a good one. A spatula with a sturdy yet flexible nylon head can be used for almost any application, whether you're flipping burgers or pancakes, or slipping snickerdoodles off a baking sheet.

Obviously, this is not a comprehensive list, just the top five, and if I expanded it to the top ten, I would include a great kitchen spoon, a grater like the Microplane zesters, a good can opener, quality kitchen shears, good quality mixing and prep bowls, and a whisk. However, the top five listed above are essential for almost every cook's kitchen.

– **Tim Wheeler** *has been the owner of the Durango Coffee Company since 2004. It is a long-standing, iconic Durango business, having been in its present location since 1990. The Durango Coffee Company consists of two interrelated businesses: a coffee bar/café and a gourmet kitchen store and has been a trusted source of information and products for cooks for over twenty years.*

appetizers

DORADO CEVICHE
The Golden Triangle

CEVICHE
2 lbs. Mahi Mahi
   or any lean white fish
10 key limes
   (regular limes will do)

2 lemons
1 Tbsp. salt

PICO DE GALLO
5 Roma tomatoes seeded and cubed
½ white onion diced
1 bunch fresh cilantro
4 fresh jalapeño peppers

This dish makes a great party item. Any lean fish or seafood will do; avoid using oily fish such as salmon, cod, or mackerel.

FOR THE CEVICHE: Dice the fish into ½-inch cubes.
In a nonreactive bowl marinate the cubed fish in the juice of the limes, the lemon and salt for at least 1 hour, to allow the acid in the citrus juice to cure the flesh of the fish.

FOR THE PICO DE GALLO: Combine tomatoes, onion, cilantro and peppers.

ASSEMBLY: Strain the marinated fish.

In a non reactive bowl, combine the drained marinated fish with the pico de gallo. Adjust the seasoning to taste with a little more salt and a couple dashes of Tabasco sauce.

Serve the ceviche in a bowl accompanied with corn tortilla chips.

MAKES 10 SERVINGS

BLUE CRAB & ARTICHOKE DIP

Norton's Catering Company

½ lb. blue crab lump meat
1½ lbs. softened cream cheese
1½ cups of ¼-inch diced celery

½ cup fine-diced, red onion
2 cups coarsely chopped artichoke heart
½ cup grated Parmesan

4 cups loosely packed, grated Swiss cheese
½ Tbsp. crushed red peppers

Mix all ingredients until just combined.

Bake for approximately 25 minutes at 350 degrees, covered.

Serve with crackers, vegetables and chips.

CRAB & SCALLOP CEVICHE

Red Snapper

¼ cup diced Serrano peppers
½ lb. pulled crab meat
   (carefully remove small pieces of shell)
½ lb. fresh sea scallops

1 avocado diced
½ cup diced tomatoes
½ cup deseeded, skinned cucumber diced

¼ cup chopped cilantro
½ cup diced red onion
Fresh lime juice

Dice up cooked and chilled crab meat. Dice up raw sea scallops. Add all remaining ingredients; just cover with fresh lime juice.

Refrigerate for 12 hours.

Serve cold with chips or crackers.

SPICY & SWEET ROSEMARY ROASTED NUTS

eno wine bar and coffee café

4 cups raw nuts (use your favorites)	4 Tbsp. real maple syrup	¼ teas. cayenne
4 Tbsp. butter	2 Tbsp. fresh rosemary, chopped fine	2 teas. coarse salt

In a large skillet, toast the nuts over medium heat, stirring occasionally so that they don't burn.

In a small saucepan, melt butter and maple syrup together. Once melted, add rosemary and cayenne.

When the nuts are toasted, pour the butter mixture over the nuts and toss to coat. Spread the glazed nuts out on a parchment-lined or nonstick baking sheet pan and roast in a 350 degree oven for 15-20 minutes until your desired level of roast.

When you take the nuts out of the oven, sprinkle with salt.

TEQUILA SHRIMP

Francisco's Restaurant

4 extra large shrimp, cleaned	½ teas. minced shallot	large pinch of minced cilantro
1 Tbsp. oil	½ cup heavy cream	½ lime, juiced
½ teas. minced garlic	2 Tbsp. tequila	

Butterfly the 4 extra large shrimp.

Heat oil in a large skillet and cook the shrimp for 2-3 minutes, until bright pink, then turn. Cook the shrimp another 2 minutes on the other side, then add minced garlic and shallots and sauté until fragrant. Add tequila (careful for flame!), reduce by two thirds, and then add heavy cream, one large pinch of minced cilantro and the lime juice.

Cook until cream reduces, and it is bubbling in the middle of the pan.

Serve garnished with avocado and more minced cilantro.

PAUL FETCHO
GEORGE BOUGHAN

Francisco's Restaurante Y Cantina was established in 1968 by Francis and Claudine Garcia. Francisco's Tequila Shrimp was created by Ted Garcia, head chef of Francisco's from 1985-2010. Ted graduated from The New England Culinary Institute of Art.

Today, our loyal culinary team consists of Paul Fetcho of Binghamton New York, Aaron Marshall of Tucson, Arizona, George Boughan of Durango, Ross Martinez and Daniel Ortega.

For decades, Francisco's has taken a great deal of pride in offering the freshest, most diverse and regionally authentic menu items. As a result, Francisco's is pleased to offer dozens of specials that change daily and seasonally in addition to the extensive regular menu. These items range from Maryland soft-shell crabs to organically-grown herbs and produce to local farm-raised beef and poultry.

EATING SEASONALLY IN SOUTHWEST COLORADO
LOCAL PRODUCE AVAILABILITY

La Plata County Harvest

PRODUCT	APRIL	MAY	JUNE	JULY	AUGUST	SEPT	OCT	NOV	DEC	JAN	FEB	MARCH
Arugula												
Asparagus												
Beets												
Carrots												
Cauliflower												
Chard												
Choy												
Collard Greens												
Eggplant												
Garlic												
Kale												
Lettuce												
Mustard Greens												
Onions/Scallions												
Peas												
Radishes												
Spinach												
Squash												
Turnips												
Beans												
Corn												
Peppers												
Potatoes												
Tomatoes												
Apples												
Grapes												
Apricots												
Cherries												
Peaches												
Pears												
Plums												
Raspberries												
Strawberries												

Legend:
- Months available for harvest under normal growing conditions
- Months available for harvest using season extension

La Plata County Extension Office

Why buy local food? The less our food has to travel from the field to our plates, the greater the benefits. We are not only eating fresh, healthful food, but also building regional food self-reliance, protecting open space and natural landscapes, investing in culture and tradition, and contributing to the local economy.

Where can you find local food?
- Farmers' Markets
- Restaurants and Grocery Stores
- Farm Stands and U-Pick Farms
- Community and School Gardens
- Our Own Backyard

soups, salads & buns

MARINATED CUCUMBER SALAD

East by Southwest

SANBAI-SU
Three flavor vinegar dressing:
2 cups seasoned rice vinegar
4 Tbsp. brown sugar
  (Can substitute white sugar)

1 teas. Hon Dashi powder
  or 1 oz. Dashi broth
  (Bonito stock powder can be found
  in the ethnic foods aisle)
¼ cup low sodium soy or tamari

SALAD
Wakame (dehydrated seaweed)
Four cucumbers, cut in half lengthwise
Toasted sesame seeds

This is a simple bright and flavorful salad that is good as a side or on its own. It's recommended to use hothouse or English cucumbers, since peeling and deseeding is not necessary. Regular cucumbers have thicker skin, and are sometimes coated with wax; they also have large seeds that need to be scraped out.

FOR THE SANBAI-SU: In a nonreactive bowl combine all the ingredients, and cover with plastic wrap. Heat for 2 minutes in the microwave oven. This is to allow the sugar and the Hon Dashi powder to dissolve thoroughly.

Cool the dressing down and reserve for future use. It will hold under refrigeration for quite a while.

FOR THE SALAD: Rehydrate 2 pinches "wakame" dehydrated seaweed found in the ethnic food aisle. Any dehydrated seaweed will do, or it can be omitted altogether.

With a sharp knife slice across the cucumber halves as thin as possible. The use of an "Asian Mandoline" makes this easier and produces the desired thin slices. In a non-reactive pan toss the sliced cucumbers with the re-hydrated seaweed.

Add enough dressing to coat well, allow to marinate for 10 minutes. Top with toasted sesame seeds and serve.

NOTE: You can add crab meat, tofu, shrimp or any desired protein to the cucumber salad.

MISO SOUP

East by Southwest

1 quart water	1 cup shaved bonito flakes	½ cup soft tofu cubes
1 two-inch piece "kombu"	½ cup white miso paste	¼ cup thinly sliced scallion
Japanese dashi kelp	¼ cup wakame dehydrated seaweed	

Bring water and kombu to a boil, turn off the flame. Add the bonito flakes and allow to steep for 10 minutes. Strain the dashi broth, and add the miso, wakame, tofu & scallions. Serve immediately.

NOTE: It is not advised to re-boil the soup once the miso is added because it will kill the beneficial live bacteria found in the miso paste.

SERGIO VERDUZCO

Chef Sergio started his culinary career in 1979 at the age of 17 working as a Commis des Cuisine at Paul Anka's Jubilation in Las Vegas, Nevada. In 1983 he graduated from the prestigious Culinary Institute of America, in Hyde Park, New York and returned to Las Vegas to attend UNLV where he graduated with a Bachelor of Science in Hotel and Restaurant Administration.

In 2002 Sergio moved to Durango, and opened the acclaimed East by Southwest sushi bar and restaurant, raising the bar in the Durango restaurant scene and quickly becoming one of Durango's top dining destinations. Not one to sit still, Chef Sergio has continued traveling in Japan and Southeast Asia which has led him to immerse himself in the cultures and flavors of Southeast Asian cuisine. His newest venture, The Golden Triangle, features the food and flavors of that rich and vibrant region and is a testament to his continued growth as a chef and restaurateur.

MIXED SEAFOOD SALAD
INSALATA DI FRUTTI DI MARE

DRESSING
¼ cup extra virgin olive oil
3 Tbsp. fresh lemon juice
½ teas. grated lemon zest
1 large clove garlic minced fine
Salt to taste
1 small pinch of red pepper flakes

SALAD
2 lbs. squid tentacles and bodies separated
and cleaned
1 lb. shrimp peeled and deveined
24 mussels, well scrubbed and debearded
1 small fennel bulb, trimmed and thinly
sliced (white part only)

5 large black cerignola olives cut off pit
and chopped coarsely
3 Tbsp. chopped fresh Italian parsley
Salt and fresh ground black pepper to taste

Butter lettuce leaves
Lemon wedges

FOR THE DRESSING: Whisk all ingredients together in a large bowl; set aside at room temperature.

FOR THE SALAD: Turn squid bodies inside out and cut into rings ¼-inch thick. Cut large squid heads in half.

Bring a saucepan of salted water to a boil. Add the shrimp and cook about 2 minutes. Using a slotted spoon remove shrimp from water and put in bowl of ice water to stop the cooking.

Drop the squid tentacles and rings into the boiling water and when water returns to a boil cook for 1 minute. Do not be tempted to cook longer as it will toughen. Remove squid and add to ice water bath.

Drain the boiling water except for approximately ½ cup. Add mussels and cook until they begin to open about 5 minutes. Remove from the heat and discard any mussels that did not open. Remove the mussels from their shells and discard the shells.

Drain the shrimp and squid well. Cut each shrimp into 3-4 pieces. Combine with the mussels, squid and the dressing along with the fennel, olives and parsley. Taste and adjust the seasoning.

TO COMPLETE: Make a bed of the lettuce leaves and spoon each serving of the seafood mixture into the center. Garnish with a lemon wedge and serve.

MAKES 8 SERVINGS

WINTHROP SALAD WITH STRAWBERRY VINAIGRETTE

HomeSlice Pizza

DRESSING
6 oz. fresh strawberries
1 teas. fresh basil
2 teas. balsamic vinegar
1 cup olive oil

1 Tbsp. sugar
½ teas. fresh lemon juice

SALAD
1 head romaine lettuce
½ cup candied walnuts
½ cup chopped, cooked bacon
½ cup crumbled bleu cheese

FOR THE DRESSING: Emulsify all vinaigrette ingredients together in blender or food processor and set aside.

FOR THE SALAD: Tear romaine lettuce into bite size pieces in large salad bowl, then sprinkle with bacon pieces, and candied walnuts. Pour desired amount of dressing over greens and toss to coat lightly. Lastly, sprinkle with crumbled bleu cheese and toss very lightly, serve immediately.

HAMBURGER BUNS

Cosmo Bar and Grill

1½ Tbsp. fresh yeast	⅓ cup granulated sugar	egg wash
1¼ cup warm milk	4¾ Tbsp. vegetable oil	(equal parts beaten egg and cream)
(microwave for about 2 minutes)	1½ teas. kosher salt	sesame seeds (lightly toasted)
2 eggs	5¼ cups unbleached bread flour	

FOR THE DOUGH: Heat milk; add to yeast, sugar and oil in 4 quart mixer bowl. Let sit for 5 minutes, then add dry ingredients and eggs. Mix on low speed for about 5 minutes. Increase speed to low-medium and mix another 2-3 minutes.

Put dough in a well greased bowl and cover with a damp towel, then place in a warm place for approximately two hours.

When dough has doubled in size, fold the dough to center (punching it down). Let dough rise again until doubled in size, about 1 hour. Repeat this step one last time, so the dough has risen 3 times - the third rise should take 30-40 minutes. After the third rise, place dough on a lightly floured surface. Cut the dough into 12 portions; they should weigh about 3.5 oz. each. Roll into balls, place on a large baking tray, then grease, and cover with plastic wrap. To form shape, place cooling/icing racks on top of plastic covered buns. Place baking tray in a warm place and let proof until buns are touching one another. Take plastic wrap off and brush with egg wash, then sprinkle with sesame seeds.

Bake at 375 degrees for 10 minutes; rotate tray and bake 5 minutes more.

MAKES 12 BUNS

CHRIS CROWL

Chris Crowl is no stranger to fine kitchens. He attended The Culinary Institute of America in Hyde Park, New York, from 1991 to 1993 and then completed a formative externship in Philadelphia at the award-winning Fountain Restaurant in the Four Seasons Hotel.

By the late 1990s, Crowl wanted a break from overseeing a kitchen and was eager to learn a new cuisine. He found a change of pace as a line cook at Aspen's Matsuhisa, which is world-renown for Nobu Matsuhisa's Japanese and world fusion cuisine. During this time, he was also awarded a certificate in the Court of Master Sommeliers. Crowl moved to Durango in 2002 to buy a house and start a family.

With nightly sushi specials, Crowl's influence is readily apparent on the Cosmo menu, but much of his impact is subtler. He's built a rapport with local growers because he believes in buying locally whenever possible. From a chef's perspective, this translates into each dish's ingredients being fresh and succulent. From a customer's perspective, it means that each item on the menu is infused with creativity and awash with flavor.

drinks & wine

FOOD & WINE PAIRING

The Wine Merchant

The conventional approach to wine and food matches is white wine with fish and poultry, and red wine with meat. While this usually works, a more finely tuned match will make both the food and the wine taste better, the whole being more than the sum of its parts.

One approach is to match big, hearty wines with rich, hearty foods, like barbecue for example. While this can be the occasion for big reds, more often an alternate approach, serving wines with a bit more acidity, is more successful. Slightly higher acidity in the wine serves to cleanse and refresh the palate.

Delicately flavored foods need similarly delicate wine, white or red, depending on the dish. Too rich or robust a wine will overwhelm the food.

A works-every-time approach is to pour wine with geographical similarities to your food. For example, wine from Tuscany is just right for foods typical of that part of Italy.

When a customer asks what to pour with a certain dish, our first question is almost always, "How is it seasoned?" because some combinations just don't work. For example, Pinot Noir, a brilliant match with most Continental seasonings, is a disaster with Asian spices or chiles.

Tricky wine matches are foods with highly acidic ingredients (citrus juice, tomatoes, vinegar), very spicy things (red or green chiles), and non-traditional wine matches (soy sauce, ginger, cilantro). Sometimes it is best to leave the corkscrew in the drawer and have a beer.

Pasta with red sauce has lots of acidity, so red wine with relatively more acidity is usually a more successful match than a big, soft, round red. Brothy or creamy sauced dishes are generally better with a crisp white.

Similarly, crisp, clean, spicy white wines, either dry or with a degree of sweet, are good matches for many Asian-styled foods.

In general, most wines with pronounced oak flavor, either red or white, are best served on their own, not with food.

Almost as important as the food and wine match is serving the wine at the correct temperature. Reds are best at cool room temperature, low- to mid-60s, and whites and roses are best 10-15 degrees cooler. Serving a wine too cold will dull the flavors.

If your menu varies widely and you want to serve only one wine, Champagne or other good quality bubbly is a great choice. Another excellent choice, not to be missed, is dry rose, especially one from Provence.

Wine and food have a natural affinity, so don't obsess about the match. The important thing is to drink what you like, keeping an open mind to try new things.

– **Eric Allen** *got his start in the wine business in California's Bay Area in the mid-1970s. Since that time, he has pulled corks in restaurants, has pounded the pavement for a wine distributor, and has taught Fort Lewis College's World of Wine class. He opened The Wine Merchant with Ron Greene in 2002.*

COLORADO WHISKEY MANHATTAN

eno wine bar and coffee café

COCKTAIL
2 oz. Stranahan's Colorado whiskey
½ oz. each - sweet, and dry vermouth
a dash of bitters
a splash of brandied cherry juice
2 brandied cherries (see recipe below)

BRANDIED CHERRIES
1½ lbs. dark, sweet cherries, pitted
scant ¼ cup sugar
¼ cup water

½ oz. fresh lemon juice
1 small cinnamon stick
¼ cup plus ½ oz. brandy

FOR THE COCKTAIL: Place all ingredients (except cherries) in a cocktail shaker with ice and shake vigorously. Strain into a martini glass and garnish with brandied cherries.

SERVES 1

FOR THE BRANDIED CHERRIES: Combine the sugar, water, lemon juice, and cinnamon stick in a medium saucepan. Bring to a boil and reduce the heat to medium-low; add the cherries and simmer for five minutes. Remove from the heat, remove the cinnamon stick, and stir in the brandy. Allow to cool completely before placing in a jar. Refrigerate for one week before serving.

HOT BUTTERED RUM

The Ore House

1 cup Mancos Valley Distillery,
Spiced Rum
1 cup (2 sticks) of unsalted butter
softened, and at room temperature

1 cup of packed brown sugar
1 whole clove, grated
(or ½ teas. ground cloves)

1 teas. whole nutmeg, grated
Pinch of kosher salt

Cream butter, brown sugar, spices and salt in stand mixer or with handheld mixer until light in color and fluffy, then divide into 4 portions in small ramekins or bowls. Butter-sugar-spice mixture can be made and refrigerated up to 1 day ahead if it is in a tightly sealed container.

Boil approximately 4 cups water. Portion the rum equally between four 10 oz. mugs. Pour boiling water into the mugs with rum. They should be ¾ full.

Immediately serve the hot mugs to your guests accompanied by one of the ramekins or small bowls of the butter-sugar-spice mixture. Instruct your guests to stir the butter-sugar-spice mixture into their mugs and enjoy!

MAKES FOUR 10-OUNCE MUGS

IRISH COFFEE

The Irish Embassy

IRISH COFFEE
2 tsp. brown sugar
2 oz. Irish whiskey
Hot coffee

WHIPPED CREAM
4 oz. heavy whipping cream
1-2 Tbsp. powdered sugar (to taste)

FOR THE IRISH COFFEE: Pour whiskey into mug. Add brown sugar and stir. Fill remainder of glass with hot coffee. Add lightly whipped cream on top.

FOR THE WHIPPED CREAM: In very clean and cold bowl use stand mixer or handheld mixer to whip heavy cream, gently increasing speed as the cream thickens. Beat just until soft peaks form, then mix in powdered sugar to taste. Be sure your cream is lightly whipped; if it's too heavy it will float into your drink. Serve over Irish coffee.

JOHN FINGLETON

The Irish Embassy Pub officially opened to a packed house July 17, 2008. The pub arose out of an unlikely partnership between a local Durangoan, Mick Ward, and an Irishman, Jim Shannon.

The search for a pub manager brought them John Fingleton, an Irishman who had managed many startup pubs from Dublin to Paris to the Caribbean to the U.S. John, like many, had not yet discovered the lure of Durango, but once he did, he never looked back.

The Irish Embassy Pub is a huge supporter of local events in Durango, and is very involved in the community. Shortly after the opening of the pub, Mick passed away while hiking. The Embassy received a huge outpouring of support from the community, and made a note of it to always try to give back. Participating in locally sponsored events, and having regular fundraising events at the pub, they firmly believe in helping their community grow.

entrees

CHICKEN & CASHEW STIR FRY

Norton's Catering Company

1 lb. boneless chicken breast cut into
   strips ½-inch thick
1 red bell pepper, julienned
½ cup toasted cashews

¼ cup peanut oil or canola
¼ Tbsp. minced garlic
¼ cup rice wine or dry sherry or port
⅓ cup hoisin sauce

1 Tbsp. sesame oil
Green onions cut into 1-inch lengths,
   for garnish

Heat peanut oil; add garlic and let sizzle. Add peppers and chicken; stir fry for 5-minutes. Add wine or sherry and hoisin sauce; cook until chicken is tender and glazed. Stir in sesame oil and cashews; top with green onions.

Serve over wild rice pilaf.

MAKES 2-3 SERVINGS

CHICKEN MARTINI

Norton's Catering Company

Flour w/pinch salt, paprika, white pepper
4 boneless chicken breasts 5-6 oz.
½ red onion diced
½ green bell pepper, julienned and diced
½ red bell pepper, julienned and diced

¼ cup black olives, sliced
¼ cup queen olives, sliced
¼ cup capers
¼ cup artichoke hearts
¼ cup olive oil

¼ cup clarified butter
1 Tbsp. chopped garlic
½ cup white wine

Pound chicken breasts lightly, then dredge in flour mixture. Heat both olive oil and butter together; add chicken sauté until lightly browned. Remove chicken, put on sheet pan, and finish in oven at 350 degrees for approximately 15-20 minutes.

To the oil mixture, add garlic, onions, diced peppers, both olives, capers and artichoke hearts. Sauté for approximately 3 minutes on mid to high heat, then add white wine and reduce by one third.

When chicken is done, pour sauce and veggies over chicken and let marinate for a few minutes, then put over pasta or rice.

MAKES 4 SERVINGS

CHUCK NORTON

A New Orleans native, Chuck moved to Ouray in 1977 and built the Bon Ton Restaurant with partner Jon Kosh. He moved to Durango in 1984 and began many restaurant ventures from Mickey Breen's at Silverpick, Norton's on Main, Buckskin Charlie's, Edelweiss Restaurant, Dalton Ranch Clubhouse Grill to Norton's To Go. Chuck started Norton's Catering in 1989 and it became a full-time venture in 1995.

Now Norton's Catering Company is housed in the Highway 3 Roadhouse, and features southern cuisine and fresh oysters. Chuck says, "It allows me to keep creating new dishes for both the Roadhouse and the Catering Company. Bon Appetite!"

SECRETS FROM THE BUTCHER BLOCK

Sunnyside Meats

People often ask me for the secret to cooking the perfect roast. The truth is, no single factor ensures a fabulous roast – instead it is achieved through a combination of steps:

Choose meats that come from ranches that are managed for the animal's health and well-being; the flavor and texture of these meats are unrivaled. In the case of pork, look for cuts that aren't injected with salt water, they're not as tender and won't cook the same as a roast that has no water added.

Be sure that you're choosing a cut that fits your recipe. For instance, if you want a roast that will be fork tender or will shred, the beef chuck roast or pork Boston butt braised in stock are best. Braising also works for leaner roasts such as rump or sirloin roasts, but these roasts will not shred as easily. If you plan to roast in a dry oven, look for a rib, loin or tenderloin roast.

Finally, the step that truly turns a roast into a masterpiece: Searing. Cooking the surface of meat at a high temperature will develop a depth and complexity of flavor that is simply divine. This occurrence was explained in the early 1900s by chemist Louis-Camille Maillard, now referred to as the Maillard Reaction. He discovered that reactions between sugars and amino acids in foods like bread, popcorn and roasted meats account for a wide range of distinctive flavors and aromas.

To effectively sear your roast, the surface of the cut needs to be dry. Allow the meat to rest at room temperature for an hour before it is seared; rub the roast liberally with seasonings. For stovetop searing, place a skillet or Dutch oven over high heat and add olive oil. Use a pan that can go from stovetop to oven and is large enough to fit all of your ingredients. When the oil is hot

enough to ripple slightly, add the seasoned roast. Allow the roast to sear until it has turned a deep golden brown; turn to sear the other surfaces. Once the roast is sufficiently caramelized, add your liquid and transfer to the oven for braising. Allow the roast to braise for 4-5 hours, add savory vegetables and small potatoes in the last hour. For oven searing follow the drying, seasoning,

and resting steps, then place your roast uncovered on a roasting sheet or in a roasting pan. Cook at 450 degrees until the outside is deep golden brown. Reduce oven temperature to 325 and continue roasting until the internal temperature of the roast reaches 125 for rare, 130 for medium rare, or 135 for medium (the temperature will continue to rise 5 to 10 degrees after the roast is removed from the oven). Allow approximately 12-15 minutes per pound cooking time, depending on desired doneness. Ovens vary, so rely on your meat thermometer and use times only as a guideline.

Let roast rest under a loose foil cover on a serving platter for 20 minutes before carving.

– **Holly Zink** *is the owner of Sunnyside Meats. Holly was raised in Durango, a fifth generation descendent of farmers, ranchers, and business owners. She was instilled with an entrepreneurial spirit and a strong connection with the western ranching tradition. While attending CU in Boulder, Colorado, Holly worked at a natural foods grocery store where she fell in love with the natural foods business, especially the meat and seafood department. After graduation, she went on to attend the meat sciences program at CSU and interned at meat processing facilities in Weld County, Colorado. In 2002, she moved back to Durango and opened Sunnyside Farms Market.*

Today, she shares her passion for everything meat with her husband, Jesse. Together they run the store and are constantly inspired by new flavors and techniques. Their selection of fresh meat and seafood has grown to include handmade sausages, smokehouse specialties, and oven-ready entrees.

RYAN LOWE

Ryan Lowe, a 26-year-old Durango native, is the chef of The Ore House, a restaurant 12 years his senior. A detour on the way to a mechanical engineering degree placed him in the kitchen, where the teachings of his mother, an amazing cook in her own right, served as all the training he would need. A chef at a steak house, Ryan has a self-proclaimed "affinity to vegetables." This local boy prefers to work with meat and produce from the region that raised him.

Established in 1972, The Ore House is one of Durango's oldest and finest restaurants, with an atmosphere that truly reflects the essence and history of southwestern Colorado. Specialties are steak, seafood, spirits and a garden fresh salad bar.

CHICKEN TARRAGON

The Ore House

1 chicken breast	2 Tbsp. clarified butter	¼ cup scallions, chopped
1 Tbsp. flour	1 oz. Sauterne wine	⅓ cup heavy whipping cream
Dash white pepper	½ cup mushrooms, chopped	Pinch of tarragon

This classic recipe has stood the test of time. It first appeared in *Specialty of the House,* a collection of recipes from Durango restaurants, published in 1979.

Skin and bone chicken breast, cut into 6 pieces, and dust in flour and white pepper.

In small skillet, melt butter and brown chicken pieces over high heat. Pour off excess butter and add wine, mushrooms and scallions. Cook until wine is reduced. Add cream and a pinch of tarragon. Cook over low heat until cream thickens like a gravy, about 2 to 3 minutes.

Serve on a bed of rice in an individual casserole dish.

SHRIMP HAWAIIAN

The Ore House

½ oz. clarified butter
7 oz. shrimp, peeled and deveined
½ cup red bell pepper, julienned

1 teas. fresh ginger, diced
5 fresh pineapple slices
1 oz. brandy

1 Tbsp. teriyaki sauce
3 Tbsp. pineapple juice

Heat a medium frying pan over high heat, add butter and bring to smoke. Add shrimp to pan and brown on one side. Flip shrimp and add ginger, bell pepper and pineapple. Once shrimp is browned on all sides, deglaze the pan. With all ingredients still in the pan, add brandy and flame the liquor. Once flame has burned out, add pineapple juice and teriyaki sauce. Turn to medium heat and simmer till the sauce has reduced to desired thickness, serve on a warm plate.

FOR SERVING: Stack shrimp, peppers, and pineapple in the center of a warm plate and cover with sauce. Garnish with curly green onion and lemon rind spears.

MISO BROILED BLACK COD "SAIKYO-YAKI"

3 lbs. black cod filet sliced on the bias into 5 oz. portions (skin on)	2 oz. sake 6 oz. sweet mirin (cooking rice wine)	2 cups white miso paste 1 cup granulated white sugar

This Miso marinade/glaze is very simple and versatile. It works great with any oily fish, such as salmon, yellow tail, sea bass, or cod. The sweetness of the miso against the richness of the fish creates an exuberant combination.

FOR THE MARINADE/GLAZE: Bring the sake and mirin to a boil over high heat. Allow to boil for at least one minute to evaporate the alcohol in the sake. Reduce the heat to low, add the miso paste and mix with a spoon until smooth. Add the sugar and continue to mix until the sugar granules dissolve. Stir constantly to avoid scorching the sauce. Remove from the fire and allow the sauce to cool down completely.

In a nonreactive container, marinate the portioned cod filet, at least overnight; however 48 hours is best for the marinade to work its magic.

FOR THE FISH: Lay the marinated filets flat on a baking tray, and broil under a medium flame for approximately 10 minutes, or until a blistered glaze forms over the top.

Serve with a side of sticky rice and cucumber salad.

MAKES 8 SERVINGS

EASY TERIYAKI CHICKEN

East by Southwest

6 cups sweet mirin	½ cup minced fresh ginger	1 white onion cut in half and caramelized
½ cup brown sugar	5 crushed fresh garlic cloves	on the broiler or grill until charred but
2 cups low sodium soy sauce		not burned

This teriyaki recipe is great for family barbecues and it is always a hit with the kids. It can be used with pork, beef, fish, or poultry.

FOR THE SAUCE: Bring the mirin to a boil and allow to boil for 3 minutes to evaporate the alcohol. Add all other ingredients and reduce the sauce on medium heat by a third. Remove sauce from fire and strain through a fine sieve. Cool the sauce down immediately and reserve for use.

FOR THE BARBECUE GRILL: (Thighs work best) In a nonreactive bowl marinate the chicken thighs for at least 2 hours.

Brush the chicken with the marinade as you grill it on low heat, until the chicken is fully cooked. (Discard any leftover marinade that has had raw chicken in it. If you want to reuse it, you must bring it back to a boil to kill any possible cross contamination.)

Serve meat with teriyaki sauce and sprinkle with toasted sesame seeds. Beef steaks, pork loins or ribs and fish can be done in the same method. Serve with a side of sticky rice and cucumber salad.

FOR THE KIDS – CHICKEN TERIYAKI NUGGETS: Cut chicken breast into cubes or nuggets, and dredge in corn starch or flour. In a sauté pan coated with canola oil, sauté the chicken nuggets until golden. Add enough teriyaki sauce to cover. Allow the sauce to reduce and thicken slightly so it coats the nuggets and the chicken is cooked thoroughly.

Serve over sticky rice, and sprinkle with toasted sesame seeds.

CHICKEN & DUMPLINGS WITH CRANBERRY COMPOTE

The Palace Restaurant

DUMPLINGS
10 oz. all purpose flour, sifted
1 Tbsp. baking powder
1 teas. sugar
1 teas. salt
⅛ cup vegetable oil
1⅓ cup 2% milk

CHICKEN AND GRAVY
3 six-oz. chicken breasts, skinless
1 quart chicken stock
4 oz. Blond Roux (recipe below)
2 oz. heavy cream
White pepper to taste

BLOND ROUX
3 oz. butter
3 oz. all purpose flour

CRANBERRY COMPOTE
2 cups cranberries, fresh or frozen
¼ cup sugar
1 oz. orange juice
1 oz. water
1 two-inch cinnamon stick

FOR THE DUMPLINGS: Combine the flour, baking powder, sugar and salt. Sift into a medium size bowl. Make a well and add the oil and milk. Mix thoroughly taking precaution not to over mix the dough. The dough will be loose, almost like a batter. Let dough rest in refrigerator for 10 minutes before steaming.

Using an ice cream scoop, scoop and drop dough onto a perforated steamer. Cover and steam for 10 minutes, remove and set on cooling racks. Let cool and reserve for later.

MAKES 12

FOR THE POACHED CHICKEN AND GRAVY: Bring chicken stock to a boil in a 4 quart saucepan. Add chicken breast and simmer for 10 minutes or until breast is cooked throughout. Remove chicken from saucepan and set aside to cool.

Return chicken stock to stove top and bring to a boil. Add blond roux slowly, bring to a boil and simmer for 10 minutes. Add cream and adjust salt and pepper. Return to a simmer.

FOR BLOND ROUX: In a small sauté pan gently melt butter. Slowly add flour stiring until all the flour is incorporated into the butter. Bring roux to a froth and cook for 2-3 minutes. Remove from heat and keep at room temperature.

TO ASSEMBLE: While gravy is simmering shred the chicken breast and place 4 oz. of meat in individual oven pans or oven crocks. Place 2-3 dumplings on top of the chicken and cover with dumpling gravy ensuring meat is totally covered and dumplings covered at least halfway in gravy. (Family style platter can also be constructed)

Place Chicken and Dumplings in a 450 degree oven for 10-12 minutes until gravy is bubbling. Serve hot with Palace Cranberry Compote.

CRANBERRY COMPOTE: In a small saucepan combine all the ingredients and slowly heat until sugars dissolve and cranberries start to soften. Reduce to a slow boil and simmer for 30 minutes stirring often. Cool in ice bath. Refrigerate.

PENNE PASTA

The Palace Restaurant

1½ oz. olive oil
1 Tbsp. garlic, chopped fine
1 Tbsp. shallot, chopped fine
1-2 pinches crushed red pepper
2-3 pinches black pepper, coarse grind
1 cup Italian plum tomatoes,
  stewed & diced (do not drain liquid)

10-12 each fresh basil leaves,
  medium size leaf, julienne cut
10 oz. penne pasta, pre-cooked
3 oz. fresh mozzarella cheese,
  ¼-inch dice

2 pinches fresh Italian parsley,
  coarsely chopped
3 pinches Parmesan or Romano cheese,
  grated
1 two-inch cinnamon stick

FOR THE PASTA: Preheat a 10-inch sauté pan or shallow saucepan over medium heat. Be careful not to overheat the pan to prevent the olive oil from burning. Add olive oil, garlic, shallots, black pepper, and crushed red pepper. Gently sauté till garlic and shallots are soft. Do not brown garlic!

Stir in plum tomatoes and basil. Simmer for 10-12 minutes stirring often. Toss in pre-cooked penne pasta. Return to simmer and heat pasta thoroughly. Adjust salt to taste.

Finish with fresh mozzarella tossed gently in the pasta. Remove pasta from pan while mozzarella is still cool and not totally melted. Garnish each serving with fresh chopped parsley and grated Parmesan or Romano cheese. Enjoy!

VARIATIONS: You can also add Italian sausage, chicken, or shrimp to this dish. Sauté these ingredients thoroughly before you add the garlic and shallots.

NOTE: Always pre-heat your serving platters, plates, or bowls in a warm oven to insure hot food when it arrives at the table.

PAUL GELOSE

Chef/Owner Paul Gelose purchased the Palace in 1997 and has turned what was a 30-year-old, but struggling, restaurant into one of the most favored dining establishments in Durango. As part of his heritage, Paul was exposed to the richness of Italian and Sicilian cuisine at an early age and acquired a passion for the kitchen in his youth. A native of upstate New York, Paul moved out West to Steamboat Springs, Colorado, in 1981, to begin what would become an extensive career in the food arts. From 1990 to 1997 he owned and operated three Telluride favorites, the Powderhouse Restaurant and Bar, Joe's Catering and Giusseppes at the Plunge. From 1996 to 1997, Paul took a break from the mountains and moved to Chicago to be Oprah Winfrey's personal chef. It was the opportunity to purchase the Palace Restaurant that brought him back to Colorado.

When he is not at the restaurant he is enjoying life in the San Juan Mountains with his wife Carolyn, and their daughter Allegra.

JOHN SHEEHAN

John Sheehan has been in the restaurant business for over 30 years. He currently owns, with his wife Nancy, a seafood and steak restaurant located in downtown Durango called The Red Snapper. John and Nancy also own an Italian restaurant located in Phoenix, Arizona called Salute's.

CIOPPINO

Red Snapper

¼ cup of diced yellow onion
½ cup of diced leeks
2 Tbsp. minced garlic
2 cups fish stock

3 bay leaves
¼ cup fresh basil
½ cup sweet vermouth

2 quarts diced whole peeled tomatoes
2 teas. crushed red pepper flakes

Assorted seafood (see recipe)

FOR THE SAUCE: Sauté garlic, onions, and leeks in olive oil. Once they are translucent, add sweet vermouth and let simmer 2-3 minutes. Add fish stock and bay leaves, and let cook for 5 minutes. Add tomatoes, red pepper flakes, and fresh basil; once brought to a boil, turn down heat and let cook on low for 20 minutes. Add salt and pepper to taste.

FOR THE SEAFOOD: (clams, callops, shrimp, white fish, etc.): Get pan hot, add a touch of oil and pan-sear your seafood. Add cioppino broth and let simmer 2-3 minutes, then serve.

IRISH STEW

The Irish Embassy

2 Tbsp. + 2 teas. chopped fresh garlic
2 Tbsp. + 2 teas. dried sage
2 Tbsp. + 2 teas. dried rosemary
2 Tbsp. + 2 teas. dried thyme
½ Tbsp. kosher salt
¾ teas. ground pepper

2½ lbs. shoulder lamb,
   cubed and trimmed
1 oz. clarified butter
1 cups carrots sliced 1 inch and cut in half
4 cups parsnips – same size as carrots
⅔ lbs. roughly chopped white onion
1 cup dry white wine

8 cups peeled potatoes,
   cut into 1-inch slices and quartered
12 cups of water
¼ box pearled barley
¼ cup flat leaf parsley chopped,
   for garnish

Preheat an 8-gallon stockpot to medium high. Mix first seven ingredients in a bowl.

When the stockpot is hot, add butter and lamb mixture. Turn cubes to ensure even browning of the lamb – about 10 minutes – don't let the meat burn. When the meat has browned, immediately remove from pot.

Add the carrots, parsnips, and an additional 2 Tbsp. of salt and 1 Tbsp. of fresh ground pepper to the stockpot. Reduce heat to medium and begin to scrape the bottom of the pot for 3-5 minutes. Add wine and deglaze and reduce slightly. Add potatoes, water, barley, and return lamb back to the stockpot. Slowly bring to a simmer, stirring occasionally. Simmer for 4-6 hours – never let it boil!

Refrigerate for 24 hours before serving. Garnish with fresh parsley.

ROMAN OXTAIL STEW
CODA ALLA VACCINARA

3 lbs. Oxtail approx. 2-3 inches thick
½ cup flour or more as needed
⅓ cup extra virgin olive oil
1 white onion finely chopped
3 oz. pancetta minced fine
2 large garlic cloves chopped

3 anchovy filets chopped
¼ cup finely chopped fresh flat-leaf parsley
1 teas. salt
½ teas. freshly ground black pepper
1 cup dry Italian red wine

2 28-oz. cans Italian plum tomatoes
    with the juice, crushed by hand
3 large celery stalks cut into 1-inch pieces
3 medium sized carrots cut into
    1-inch pieces

Preheat oven to 350 degrees.

Salt and pepper oxtail then flour, shaking off excess. Heat oil in large ovenproof skillet; add the oxtail in batches taking care not to crowd the pan. Remove oxtail and add onion, pancetta, garlic, anchovy and parsley to the skillet, cook until golden. Do not burn garlic.

Return oxtail to the pan and raise the heat to high and add the wine, scraping the bottom of the pan until the wine is reduced by half. Add the tomatoes and bring to a boil. Cover with a tight fitting lid and place in preheated oven.

Cook for 1.5 hours stirring a few times during cooking. Add celery and carrots and cook another 1.5 to 2 hours until the meat is falling away from the bone. If the sauce becomes too thick add some warm water.

Serve in individual serving bowls.

MAKES 6 SERVINGS

RISOTTO WITH PORCINI MUSHROOMS & SMOKED PROSCIUTTO
RISOTTO ALL BOSCAIOLA

Guido's

6-8 cups meat stock (homemade is best) or low sodium canned stock	5 Tbsp. butter	1 cup dry, full bodied, red wine
1 oz. dried porcini mushrooms, soaked in 2 cups lukewarm water for 20 minutes (undisturbed the last 5 minutes of soaking)	1 small onion finely minced	2 Tbsp. finely chopped fresh Italian parsley
	2 cups imported Italian carnaroli rice	1 cup freshly grated reggiano parmigiano cheese
	3 oz. prosciutto speck cut into sliced and diced	

Heat the broth in saucepan and keep warm over low heat. Carefully lift mushrooms out of soaking liquid trying not to disturb soaking water. Rinse the mushrooms under cold water. Line a strainer with two layers of paper towels or coffee filter and strain the soaking liquid into a bowl to get rid of the grit. Set aside.

Melt 4 Tbsp. of the butter in large saucepan over medium heat. Add the onion and cook stirring until it is soft 5-7 minutes. Add the rice and cook until it is well coated with the butter about 3 minutes. Add the speck and mushrooms and stir a minute or so. Add the wine and cook stirring constantly until the wine has evaporated. Add 1 cup of the reserved mushroom liquid and cook until it is almost all reduced. Add just enough stock to cover and cook until it is reduced almost completely. Continue adding broth and reducing for 25 minutes or until the rice is tender but still firm to the bite. At the last reduction of broth do not reduce completely so that the rice will have a moist creamy consistency. Stir in the remaining butter and ⅓ cup of cheese. Serve at once passing the remaining cheese at the table.

MAKES 6 SERVINGS

TAGLIATELLE WITH LEONIDA'S SAUCE
TAGLIATELLE CON LA SALSA DI LEONIDA

4 Tbsp. unsalted butter
1 small onion finely minced
1 small to medium carrot finely minced
1 large garlic clove finely minced
¼ lb. pancetta diced

1 cup dry white wine
3 Tbsp. tomato paste mixed with 2 cups
   chicken broth (preferably homemade)
   or canned low sodium stock

Salt and fresh ground black pepper
2 Tbsp. heavy cream
½ teas. freshly grated nutmeg
1 cup reggiano parmigiano cheese
   freshly grated

FOR THE SAUCE: Heat the butter over medium low heat. Add the carrot and cook 4-5 minutes; add the onion and cook an additional 4-5 minutes. Add the pancetta and cook until the pancetta is golden. Add the garlic and stir a few times (about a minute). Add the wine and cook on high heat until the wine is reduced by half. Add the tomato paste and broth; cook uncovered 10 minutes on medium to low heat stirring a few times. During the last minute of cooking add the cream and the nutmeg.

TO SERVE: Serve over tagliatelle noodles cooked using the package instructions. Top generously with parmigiano cheese. Homemade noodles with make this dish shine!

MAKES 6 SERVINGS

SUSAN DEVEREAUX

Susan has always had a passion for cooking beginning at a very young age. She is well traveled and always seeks out new foods to taste and experience. She lived in Italy where the ingredients are fresh and preparations are simple. Italian cooking became her passion, especially Trattoria style cooking which is what is offered at Guido's.

Susan is a retired stockbroker now, restaurant owner and chef. Cooking as a hobby became a full-time rewarding job where she now cooks daily. She still travels to Italy each year with Guido (alias Sean Devereaux) and Guido's chefs in order to maintain and increase the level of their culinary skills. Food diaries are kept during these visits. Food is her obsession.

ALISON DANCE & VERA HANSEN

Alison Dance loves good food, good wines, good music and art. Her Cyprus Café and new addition, eno wine bar and coffee café, are a joyous expression of all these.

Chef Vera Hansen and Alison create seasonal dishes that are simple, healthy, and tasty in this restaurant "where the Mediterranean meets the Mountains." Cyprus Café uses local organic produce and meats and sustainably harvested seafood whenever possible to create meals that are as delicious as they are beautiful. Their meals fuse the best of Italian, Greek, North African and Southwest American flavors.

Dance and Hansen have been working together for 15 years, almost since the day Cyprus Café opened back in 1996. Together, they have developed a unique palate of flavors and foods that turn first timers into devoted patrons of food, wine, and the arts.

HARISSA GRILLED LAMB SHISHKEBAB

SHISHKEBAB	HARISSA	COUSCOUS
1-1½ lbs. cleaned leg of lamb	¼ cup cumin seeds	2 cups dry couscous
red bell pepper, cut into 1" to 2"pieces	¼ cup coriander seeds	½ cup toasted almonds rough chopped
red onion cut into 1" to 2" pieces	¼ cup paprika	½ cup dried apricots rough chopped
½ cup Harissa	1 teas. cayenne	4 Tbsp. chopped herbs
½ cup olive oil	1 teas. salt	(rosemary, thyme, basil, parsley…)
salt and pepper		2 cups hot stock, chicken or vegetable

FOR THE LAMB: Mix dried Harissa powder (directions below) and olive oil together. Toss lamb in mixture and let sit for at least two hours. You can let this sit overnight if you'd like the Harissa flavor to permeate the meat.

Using at least 8-inch metal or bamboo skewers, alternate lamb, red pepper and onion on skewer. Chargrill or roast in oven until done to your liking. Serve over Almond and Herb Couscous.

FOR THE HARISSA: In large frying pan, place cumin and coriander seeds, paprika and cayenne. Toast until seeds pop, being careful not to burn. Grind fine in spice grinder and add salt to taste.

TOASTED ALMOND, DRIED APRICOT & HERB COUSCOUS: In a medium sized metal bowl toss couscous, apricots, herbs and almonds. Add hot stock and stir to blend all ingredients. Immediately cover the bowl with a piece of plastic wrap to seal. Let couscous rest for about 10 minutes or until all the stock has been absorbed. Remove plastic wrap and fluff with a fork and serve.

MAKES 4 SERVINGS

ENCHILADAS

Zia Taqueria

ENCHILADA SAUCE	CHICKEN	TORTILLAS
¼ lb. Guajillo chiles	2 lbs. chicken breast	30 white corn tortillas
3 tomatoes	Pinch of salt	3 cups vegetable or canola oil
1½ garlic cloves	Pinch of black pepper	
¼ white onion		1 lb. of Monterey jack or cheddar cheese
Pinch of cumin		
Pinch of cinnamon		

This recipe is one of Zia Taqueria customers' favorite daily specials. Please allow a couple of hours for prep time. Enjoy. This recipe yields one pan of enchiladas.

FOR THE SAUCE: Put all of the enchilada sauce ingredients in a large pan and fill with enough water to cover all the ingredients. Boil until the tomatoes are soft. Strain out about half the water and then puree ingredients into a nice smooth sauce. Pour the sauce through a strainer into a saucepan to remove all the pepper seeds. Hold sauce on low heat until it is time to add to the enchiladas.

FOR THE CHICKEN: In a large pot, boil the chicken until the meat is easily pulled apart with tongs. Add the salt and pepper for flavor. Once chicken is cooked, strain the chicken but be sure to save the stock to make yourself some delicious Posole soup. Finely shred the chicken with tongs.

FOR THE TORTILLAS: In a large sauté pan, flash fry all the tortillas in the oil for about 30 seconds. And then transfer to a large hotel pan.

TO ASSEMBLE: Preheat oven to 350 degrees.

Place approximately 1½ oz. of shredded chicken into each tortilla, roll up the tortillas filled with chicken into enchiladas, and then place them in a large hotel pan. Place rolled up enchiladas into three rows with ten enchiladas in each row. Cover enchiladas completely with sauces and then spread cheese evenly over the top. Place enchiladas in oven and bake for about 30 minutes or until internal temperature is 165 degrees.

MAKES 30 ENCHILADAS

ZIA'S CREW

In the spring of 2005, Tim Turner and his wife Becky opened a fresh-food Mexican restaurant (fresh-mex) on the north end of Durango. Their goal was to offer healthy and fresh food at a reasonable price, in a clean and hip environment, with an eye toward supporting a local, living economy. It sounds like a mouthful, but it's all quite simple, as are most things in life, and that is how the Zia crew likes to keep it: tasty, fresh, local, simple, and clean, served with a sincere smile.

Zia is proud to be in a position to give back to the community that has allowed for its success and extends its humble and gracious thank you to all. Buen Provecho.

KARMA TENZING BHOTIA

Executive chef Karma Tenzing Bhotia is delighted to bring his unique cuisine to southwest Colorado, at the Himalayan Kitchen. Karma was born and raised in the remote Mt. Makalu region of northeast Nepal. As a certified mountain guide and semi-professional photographer, Karma has traveled extensively throughout the Himalayas. His travels helped him learn the nuances of Himalayan cooking, a cuisine that utilizes black and white cardamon, jimbu, garlic, ginger, cumin, coriander, star anis, timboor, chili, turmeric, saffron, sesame and mustard seed. Karma spent several years as a chef in Austria, enabling him to combine the bold flavors from his homeland of Nepal with the subtleties of European cuisine. Karma uses his expertise in Himalayan and European cooking along with fresh herbs and spices to create unique flavors in every dish.

CHAANA TARKARI
GARBANZO BEAN CURRY
The Himalayan Kitchen

2 cans (16 oz.) garbanzo beans,
   drained and rinsed
3 medium boiled potatoes peeled and
   cut into 1x1 inch cube
1 whole chopped onion
2 chopped tomatoes

2 cloves of minced garlic
1 Tbsp. of minced ginger
½ teas. crushed chili
   (according to how spicy you like)
1 teas. salt
¼ teas. turmeric

1 Tbsp. curry powder
1 Tbsp. olive oil
4 cups vegetable broth
½ cup diced green onion
½ cup chopped cilantro

Heat the pot and add oil. Then add the onion and sauté until browned. Add garlic, ginger, chili, and turmeric. Add the tomatoes, salt and curry powder and simmer for 2 minutes. Now add the garbanzo beans, vegetable broth, green onion and cilantro. Cook for 5 minutes, then add the boiled potatoes and cook for 5 minutes. Now your Chaana Tarkari is ready to serve.

Serve with basmati rice or naan.

CUMIN BRINED PORK TENDERLOIN WITH PEPITA SAUCE

Sow's Ear

CUMIN BRINE
1 quart water
⅛ cup salt
⅛ cup sugar
¼ cup cumin seeds
1 bay leaf
½ Tbsp. black peppercorns
2 sprigs fresh thyme

PORK
2 lbs. pork tenderloin, silver skin removed

PEPITA SAUCE
½ cup toasted pepitas (pumpkin seeds)
¼ white onion, chopped
2 garlic cloves
½ cup chicken stock
¼ cup cilantro
½ cup chicken stock
Juice of one lime

PICKLED ONIONS
1 cup apple cider vinegar
1 bay leaf
¼ cup sugar
½ Tbsp. coriander seed
1 teas. black peppercorns

1 red onion

FOR THE BRINE: Bring all ingredients to a boil, simmer five minutes and cool.

Marinate pork in cooled cumin brine for 8-12 hours.

FOR THE PEPITA SAUCE: Puree pepitas, onion, garlic and stock in blender. Pour into saucepan and simmer five minutes or until sauce thickens. Return to blender and add cilantro, stock and lime juice. Salt and pepper to taste. Keep warm.

FOR PICKLED ONIONS: Simmer all ingredients for five minutes. Cool and add one red onion, thinly sliced. Let onions marinate for at least an hour.

TO SERVE: Remove pork from brine and grill to desired temperature. Top with pepita sauce and the pickled onions removed from the pickling juice.

Serve with chipotle mashed potatoes and garnish with fresh cilantro.

GEORGE MEHAFFIE

The Sow's Ear Restaurant, established in 1986, is located in the Silverpick Lodge, just one mile south of Durango Mountain Resort in the beautiful San Juan Mountains.

The Sow's Ear is the longest running restaurant in the area with new owner and chef George Mehaffie taking over in May of 2008. While continuing the tradition of "The Best Steaks on the Mountain," he has brought a seasonal feel to the menu, including the popular addition of small plates and new light fare.

BRENDAN BALLO

Brendan Ballo started in the restaurant business when he was just a teenager. Working in a family owned restaurant, Brendan started as the dishwasher and worked his way up to sous chef, and has been in the restaurant industry ever since. Brendan was the sous chef at Stewarts Cafe in New Jersey, and also the sous chef at Off Belleview Grille in Denver. He moved to Durango in 2003 and quickly became the executive chef at Randy's, where he has been for almost seven years.

Brendan's culinary goal is to challenge restaurant goers with bold flavors, and contrasts in texture and temperature. He also engages diners by using local products in "amuse bouche" cuisine. These small bites, "amuse the mouth" and allow the customer an opportunity to taste a wide variety of culinary creations. Brendan is continuously evolving as a chef by incorporating new techniques and styles. One day, Brendan wishes to open a small high-end restaurant of his own.

MARINATED TENDERLOIN FILET
WITH RANDY'S APPLE ONION PUREE AND RANDY'S GRUYERE POTATO HASH

Randy's Restaurant

MARINADE
1 cup apple cider vinegar
2 Tbsp. hazelnut oil

BEEF
4, 6-oz. tenderloin beef filets

RAISIN STOCK
1 cup raisins
1 bay leaf
10 peppercorns
2 peeled garlic cloves
1 cinnamon stick
1 quart water

APPLE ONION PUREE
3 green apples, peeled, cored, and diced
1 yellow onion peeled, and roughly chopped
2 Tbsp. butter
1 Tbsp. xanthan gum
   (you can purchase at natural food stores)
Salt and pepper to taste

POTATO HASH
1 whole yam (approx. 14 oz.)
   peeled and shredded
2 strips apple wood smoked bacon,
   julienned
1 cup shredded gruyere
½ cup bourbon
1 Tbsp. unsalted butter
¼ cup chopped green onion

1 Tbsp. hazelnut oil
1 Tbsp. granulated sugar
4 fresh fennel fronds

FOR THE MARINADE: Whisk together hazelnut oil and apple cider vinegar in a large bowl. Marinate the steaks in the vinegar and oil for no less than 4 hours. Once the steaks are marinated, salt and pepper them to taste, then Chargrill to desired temperature.

FOR THE APPLE ONION PUREE: In large pot combine all ingredients for Raisin Stock, boil and reduce to 1½ cups of liquid, set aside.

Sauté apples and onions in a pot until they are soft. With emulsion blender or food processor slowly add stock to sautéed apple and onions, puree until smooth and desired consistency. Add 1 Tbsp. of xanthan gum and salt and pepper to taste. Set aside until ready to plate with steaks and hash.

FOR THE POTATO HASH: Begin by cooking bacon on medium heat. When cooked about 3/4 of the way through, deglaze pan with bourbon and add butter (be careful of flame). Next add shredded yam and cook for about five minutes on low heat. Finally, add the gruyere and green onion and put aside to plate with Randy's filet and Apple Onion Puree.

FOR SERVING: Pour ¼ cup of apple puree into the center of the plate. Offset ¼ of the potato hash and top with chargrilled filet. Sprinkle the plate with a little bit of the hazelnut oil then sprinkle with ¼ of sugar and top meat with fresh fennel fronds. Repeat with remaining steaks.

desserts

DARK CHOCOLATE LOVE CAKE
[FLOURLESS & GLUTEN FREE]

Celebration Cakes

| 16 oz. (1 pound) bittersweet chocolate | 5 eggs at room temperature | ⅓ cup, plus 1 Tbsp. unsweetened cocoa |
| 4 oz. (1 stick) no salt butter | ⅔ cup fine granulated sugar | |

IN PREPARATION: Preheat oven to 375 degrees. Boil enough water for a water-bath. Grease a springform pan and dust with cocoa.

FOR THE CAKE: Melt chocolate and butter. Set aside to cool down.

Beat eggs. Sprinkle with sugar and continue beating until light in color. Fold in the cocoa (keeping air in previous mixture).

Incorporate cooled chocolate with egg mixture. Scrape into springform pan wrapped in foil around base and sides.

Place pan in a recently boiled water-bath. Carefully place in pre-heated oven and turn down to 350 degrees. Check at 25 to 30 minutes. Cake will be done when firm. Cool slowly. Chill for transfer to serving plate.

OPTIONAL TOPPING: Pourable melted chocolate over top.

HEATHER HINSLEY

Celebration Cakes specializes in custom quality desserts that are made fresh in a local commercial kitchen. As owner and artist, Heather Hinsley, personally ensures both professional taste and appearance in each creation. Heather gives credit to her aunt from Sicily, Angelina, for passionate inspiration. Heather's experience includes apprenticeships with the finest pastry chefs, complementing her Bachelor's Degree in Art Education.

Cake is a form of celebration in the field of culinary arts. From the moment of mixing to the end design, each order is a custom work of art. The edible art has local ingredients such as flour, eggs and other dairy whenever possible, to enhance flavor and support our community of the Four Corners.

CHOCOLATE MOUSSE

8 oz. high-quality, bittersweet chocolate chips	4 large egg yolks ½ cup heavy cream 3 Tbsp. sugar 1 teas. vanilla	1½ cups heavy cream, cold

Melt chocolate in a double boiler or a metal bowl set over a pan of simmering water.

While chocolate is melting, prepare the egg yolks, heavy cream and sugar. Whisk well until combined. Heat, stirring constantly, until 150 degrees. Remove from heat and stir in vanilla.

Combine melted chocolate with cream mixture. Let cool.

Whip remaining heavy cream just to stiff peaks.

Fold ½ of whipped cream into chocolate mixture until smooth. Fold remaining cream in, just until incorporated. Spoon into serving dishes, cover and chill for at least 6 hours and up to 24 hours.

Top with additional sweetened whipped cream if desired.

ROBERT ZIEGLER

Never subjected to formal training, Robert has learned his craft in many small bakeries from Olympia, Washington, to Louisville, Kentucky. Owning his own bakery is the fulfillment of a lifelong dream, and could never have been achieved without the help and inspiration of his wife Kelly.

Robert is proud to be part of the Durango community as he looks forward to many more years of successful baking.

CHOCOLATE CHIP COOKIES

Serious Delights

6 oz. butter, plus 2 ounces butter	1 teas. vanilla extract	½ teas. baking soda
9 oz. sugar	2 eggs	9 oz. chocolate chips
1 Tbsp. molasses	9 oz. bread flour	

Melt 6 ounces of butter on stovetop. Cook until lightly browned. Brown butter until covered with foam and butter is as dark as honey. Remove from heat, let cool for a few minutes. Stir in remaining 2 ounces of butter until melted. Pour melted butter into mixing bowl.

Add sugar, molasses and vanilla to melted butter. Beat on first speed for 30 seconds. Rest one minute.

Add eggs. Beat and rest again twice more, until thick, smooth and satiny.

Sift dry ingredients together and then add to mixer. Gently fold into batter on first speed, just until combined.

Stir into batter until well mixed. Scoop cookies, as desired, onto baking sheet. Bake at 350 degrees until dark golden brown. Our oven works differently than home ovens, but we bake the cookies for 18-20 minutes.

BLACK CURRANT SORBET

The Ore House

3 cups granulated sugar	4 cups black currant juice	Juice from one fresh lemon
3 cups plus 2 Tbsp. water	1 Tbsp. cornstarch	Zest from one fresh lemon

In a medium saucepan combine sugar and 3 cups water. Place over medium heat and cook till the sugar has completely dissolved. Add black currant juice and mix thoroughly. Bring the sugar, water and juice mixture to a simmer.

Meanwhile, combine the remainder of the water with the cornstarch to create a slurry.

Once the currant mixture is simmering, slowly mix in the slurry continuing to stir occasionally for 5 minutes. Remove the pan from heat and add lemon juice and zest.

Pour the contents into an ice cream maker and freeze. Once frozen, reserve in freezer for later or serve.

INDEX